D0374947

BACKYARD WILDLIFE

Coyotes

by Emily Green

BLASTOFF! READERS

BELLWETHER MEDIA • MINNEAPOLIS, MN

Note to Librarians, Teachers, and Parents:

Blastoff! Readers are carefully developed by literacy experts and combine standards-based content with developmentally appropriate text.

Level 1 provides the most support through repetition of high-frequency words, light text, predictable sentence patterns, and strong visual support.

Level 2 offers early readers a bit more challenge through varied simple sentences, increased text load, and less repetition of high-frequency words.

Level 3 advances early-fluent readers toward fluency through increased text and concept load, less reliance on visuals, longer sentences, and more literary language.

Level 4 builds reading stamina by providing more text per page, increased use of punctuation, greater variation in sentence patterns, and increasingly challenging vocabulary.

Level 5 encourages children to move from "learning to read" to "reading to learn" by providing even more text, varied writing styles, and less familiar topics.

Whichever book is right for your reader, Blastoff! Readers are the perfect books to build confidence and encourage a love of reading that will last a lifetime!

This edition first published in 2011 by Bellwether Media, Inc.

No part of this publication may be reproduced in whole or in part without written permission of the publisher. For information regarding permission, write to Bellwether Media, Inc., Attention: Permissions Department, 5357 Penn Avenue South, Minneapolis, MN 55419.

Library of Congress Cataloging-in-Publication Data
Green, Emily K., 1966–
Coyotes / by Emily Green.
    p. cm. – (Blastoff! readers: Backyard wildlife)
Includes bibliographical references and index.
Summary: "Developed by literacy experts for students in kindergarten through grade three, this book introduces coyotes to young readers through leveled text and related photos"–Provided by publisher.
    ISBN 978-1-60014-439-4 (hardcover : alk. paper)
    1. Coyote–Juvenile literature. I. Title.
QL737.C22G7245 2010
599.77'25–dc22   2010006431

Text copyright © 2011 by Bellwether Media, Inc. BLASTOFF! READERS and associated logos are trademarks and/or registered trademarks of Bellwether Media, Inc.

Printed in the United States of America, North Mankato, MN.

080110   1162

Contents

Coyotes are a type of **wild** dog. They are also called prairie wolves.

Most coyotes have brown, gray, or yellow fur.

Coyotes have bushy tails with black tips.

Coyotes have yellow eyes and pointed ears. They also have sharp teeth.

Coyotes eat berries, grass, and **insects**.

Coyotes also eat small animals like birds, rabbits, and mice. Coyotes are good hunters.

Coyotes live in forests, prairies, and deserts.

Most coyotes live in **packs**. A pack has between three and six coyotes.

Coyotes bark, **yip**, and **howl**. They howl to call their packs together. Aaaaoooooo!

Glossary

howl–a loud, long, sad sound

insects–small animals with six legs and hard outer bodies; insect bodies are divided into three parts.

packs–groups of the same kind of animal that live together

wild–living in nature

yip–a short bark or cry

To Learn More

AT THE LIBRARY

Hiscock, Bruce. *Coyote and Badger: Desert Hunters of the Southwest*. Honesdale, Pa.: Boyds Mills Press, 2001.

Hodge, Deborah. *Wild Dogs: Wolves, Coyotes, and Foxes*. Tonawanda, N.Y.: Kids Can Press, 1997.

Webster, Christine. *Coyotes*. New York, N.Y.: Weigl, 2008.

ON THE WEB

Learning more about coyotes is as easy as 1, 2, 3.

1. Go to www.factsurfer.com.

2. Enter "coyotes" into the search box.

3. Click the "Surf" button and you will see a list of related Web sites.

With factsurfer.com, finding more information is just a click away.

Index

The images in this book are reproduced through the courtesy of: Geoffrey Kuchera, front cover, p. 5; Denis Pepin, p. 7; Michael Sedam/Photolibrary, p. 9; Juan Martinez, pp. 11, 17 (left, middle, right); Richard Wear/Photolibrary, p. 13; Vakrushev Pavel, p. 13 (left); Yuriy Kulyk, p. 13 (middle); Andrey Pavlov, p. 13 (right); Visuals Unlimited/Masterfile, p. 15; Russell Shively, p. 15 (left): Eduard Kyslynskyy, p. 15 (right); Bev McConnell, p. 17; Jianchun Zhang, p. 19; John J. Henderson, p. 21.